Managing the Impact of Wildfires on Communities and the Environment

*A Report to the President
In Response to the Wildfires of 2000
September 8, 2000*

I. Executive Summary

On August 8, 2000, President Clinton asked Secretaries Babbitt and Glickman to prepare a report that recommends how best to respond to this year's severe fires, reduce the impacts of these wildland fires on rural communities, and ensure sufficient firefighting resources in the future.

The President also asked for short-term actions that Federal agencies, in cooperation with States, local communities and Tribes, can take to reduce immediate hazards to communities in the wildland-urban interface and to ensure that land managers and firefighter personnel are prepared for extreme fire conditions in the future.

This report recommends a Fiscal Year (FY) 2001 budget for the wildland fire programs of the Departments of Agriculture and the Interior of $2.8 billion. Included within this total is an increase of nearly $1.6 billion above the President's FY 2001 budget request in support of the report's recommendations. This includes additional funding of about $340 million for fire preparedness resources, new funding of $88 million to increase cooperative programs in support of local communities, and approximately $390 million for fuels treatment and burned area restoration. The increase also includes about $770 million to replenish and enhance the Departments' fire suppression accounts, which have been depleted by this year's extraordinary costs, and to repay FY 2000 emergency transfers from other appropriations accounts.

A summary of the key points discussed in the body of the report:

1. Continue to Make All Necessary Firefighting Resources Available. The wildfires of the summer of 2000 continue to burn. As conditions change, new fires will start as others are controlled or die out. As a first priority, the Departments will continue to provide all necessary resources to ensure that firefighting efforts protect life and property. The Nation's wildland firefighting organization is the finest in the world and deserves our strong support.

2. Restore Landscapes and Rebuild Communities. The Departments will invest in restoration of communities and landscapes impacted by the 2000 fires. Some communities already have suffered considerable economic losses as a result of the fires. These losses will likely grow unless immediate, emergency action is taken to reduce further resource damage to soils, watersheds, and burned over landscapes. Key actions include:

- **Rebuilding communities and assessing economic needs.** Assess the economic needs of communities and, consistent with current authorities, commit the financial resources necessary to assist individuals and communities in rebuilding their homes, businesses, and neighborhoods. Existing loan and grant programs administered by the Federal Emergency Management Agency (FEMA), the Small Business Administration (SBA), and USDA's Forest Service and rural development programs should provide this assistance.

- **Restoring damaged landscapes.** Invest in landscape restoration efforts such as tree planting, watershed restoration, and soil stabilization and revegetation. In so doing, priority should focus on efforts to protect:

  - Public health and safety (e.g. municipal watersheds);
  - Unique natural and cultural resources (e.g. salmon and bulltrout habitat) and burned-over lands that are susceptible to the introduction of non-native invasive species; and
  - Other environmentally sensitive areas where economic hardship may result from a lack of re-investment in restoring damaged landscapes (e.g. water quality impacts on recreation and tourism).

3. **Invest in Projects to Reduce Fire Risk.** Addressing the brush, small trees, and downed material that have accumulated in many forests because of past management activities, especially a century of suppressing wildland fires, will require significant investments to treat landscapes through thinning and prescribed fire. Since 1994, the Forest Service and the Bureau of Land Management have increased the number of acres treated to reduce fuel build-up from fewer than 500,000 acres in 1994 to more than 2.4 million acres this year. Building on the forest policies of the past eight years, the wildland fire policy, and the concepts of ecosystem management, the Departments should establish a collaborative effort to expedite and expand landscape-level fuel treatments. Important dimensions of this effort include:

   ❑ **Developing a locally led, coordinated effort between the Departments of Agriculture, the Interior, and Commerce, and other appropriate agencies through the establishment of integrated fuels treatment teams at the regional and field levels.** The role of each team would be to identify and prioritize projects targeted at communities most at risk, coordinate environmental reviews and consultations, facilitate and encourage public participation, and monitor and evaluate project implementation. Each team will work closely with local communities to identify the best fit for each community.

   ❑ **Utilizing small diameter material and other biomass.** Develop and expand markets for traditionally underutilized small diameter wood and other biomass as a value added outlet for excessive fuels that have been removed.

   ❑ **Allocating necessary project funds.** Commit resources to support planning, assessments, and project reviews to ensure that hazardous fuels management is accomplished expeditiously and in an environmentally sound manner.

4. Work Directly with Communities. Working with local communities is a critical element in restoring damaged landscapes and reducing fire hazards near homes and communities. To accomplish this, the Departments recommend:

- ❑ **Expanding community participation.** Expand the participation of local communities in efforts to reduce fire hazards and the use of local labor for fuels treatment and restoration work.

- ❑ **Increasing local capacity.** Improve local fire protection capabilities through financial and technical assistance to State, local, and volunteer firefighting efforts.

- ❑ **Learning from the public.** Encourage grass roots ideas and solutions best suited to local communities for reducing wildfire risk. Expand outreach and education to homeowners and communities about fire prevention through use of programs such as Firewise.

5. Be Accountable. Establish a Cabinet-level coordinating team to ensure that the actions recommended by the Departments receive the highest priority. The Secretaries of Agriculture and the Interior should co-chair this team. Integrated management teams in the region should take primary responsibility for implementing the fuels treatment, restoration, and preparedness program. The Secretaries should assess the progress made in implementing these action items and provide periodic reports to the President.

II. Background

The 2000 fire season is undoubtedly one of the most challenging on record. Wildfires are on pace to break decades-old records. As of early September, more than 6.5 million acres – more than two times the ten-year national average -- have burned. The intensity of this year's fires is the result of two primary factors: a severe drought, accompanied by a series of storms that produced millions of lightning strikes and windy conditions, and the long-term effects of more than a century of aggressively suppressing all wildfires, which has led to an unnatural buildup of brush and small trees in our forests and rangelands.

This season has stretched the capabilities of the wildland firefighting system -- stretched, but not broken. Such a season tests our firefighters' training and the fire management infrastructure, and we have found that both are sound. This is a credit to the Nation's firefighters, support personnel, military and international partners, managers, and local communities who provide crucial help and resources.

More than 29,000 people have been involved in firefighting efforts, including about 2,500 Army soldiers and Marines and fire managers from Canada, Australia, Mexico and New Zealand. Our partners, both military and international, are assisting under pre-existing agreements with the National Interagency Fire Center in Boise, Idaho. In addition, 1,200 fire engines, 240 helicopters, and 50 airtankers are in use this season.

As challenging as this fire season has been, our firefighters have been successful in extinguishing more than 95 percent of wildfires before they become large fires (i.e., 100 acres or more). In all, they have extinguished more than 75,000 wildfire starts this season.

Weather

The weather phenomenon known as La Nina, characterized by unusually cold Pacific Ocean temperatures, changed normal weather patterns when it formed two years ago. It caused severe, long-lasting drought across much of the country, drying out our forests and rangelands. The situation was exacerbated by the fact that the drought followed several seasons of higher-than-normal rain, which fueled the growth of grasses and other plants that quickly dried when the rains stopped. This left millions of acres susceptible to fires. To make matters worse, this weather pattern also spawned a series of mostly dry thunderstorms with heavy lightning across the West. Because of the drought conditions, lightning strikes have ignited more new fires than would normally be associated with such storms.

The current season corresponds to a historical pattern of extensive wildfires during similar unusual weather conditions. The result has been an extended, severe fire season, with wildfires burning simultaneously across the western United States.

Historic wildfires

This year's fires also reflect a longer-term disruption in the natural fire cycle that has increased the risk of catastrophic fires in our forests and rangelands.

Natural fire patterns were first disrupted on a large scale with settlement activity during the second half of the 19th century when millions of acres of forests and wildlands were cleared to make way for farm crops and livestock pastures. During this time, timber companies, responding to a growing country's need for lumber and fuel, often took the biggest trees, leaving behind slash, undergrowth and smaller trees. These activities set the stage for disastrous fires.[1]

One of the most significant examples of this phenomenon occurred in 1871 in Peshtigo, Wisconsin, near the Great Lakes. The area around Peshtigo, mostly private land, had been extensively logged. Merchantable timber was removed; slash and dense undergrowth were left behind. On October 8, 1871, a brush fire quickly erupted into an inferno, consuming Peshtigo in an hour and damaging 16 other towns and more than 1.2 million acres. The human toll -- more than 1,200 people killed -- stands as the worst wildfire disaster in U.S. history.[2]

The Peshtigo tragedy served as a deadly warning about what can happen when forest health is badly compromised -- in this case, by logging activities. In fact, Peshtigo represented the beginning of new fire cycle throughout the Great Lakes region that would not be broken for more than 50 years.

In the West, a similar pattern erupted in August 1910 with the "Big Blowup" -- the Great Idaho fire. As in the 2000 fire season, a severe drought plagued the region when dry storms, accompanied by hurricane-force wind, produced thousands of lightning strikes and ignited hundreds of small fires. These fires converged to create a monster fire that was virtually unstoppable given the limited firefighting capability of the times. It consumed 3 million acres in northern Idaho and western Montana, killed 85 people, and destroyed the property and livelihoods of many others.

---

1 Stephen J. Pyne, *Fire in America: Cultural History of Wildland and Rural Fire*, Princeton University Press, 1982.
2 Green Bay Press-Gazette, from Peshtigo, Wisconsin Web Page

Speaking about the Big Blowup, Stephen Pyne, a professor at Arizona State University and a leading authority on the history of fire, said, "August of 1910 was the single most important moment in American fire history" because it radically changed the way the country viewed wildfires.[3]

The ferocity of the Big Blowup, which came on the heels of other devastating fires on both private and government land, triggered a call for a systemic policy change. Less than a year later, the national Forest Service firefighting program was born. A war on all wildfires was declared. From that point on, all wildfires were extinguished as soon as possible.

Results of suppression policy

As a result of the all-out effort to suppress fires, the annual acreage consumed by wildfires in the lower 48 states dropped from 40 to 50 million acres a year in the early 1930s to about 5 million acres in the 1970s. During this time, firefighting budgets rose dramatically and firefighting tactics and equipment became increasingly more sophisticated and effective.

While the policy of aggressive fire suppression appeared to be successful, it set the stage for the intense fires that we see today. Full suppression of all wildfires initially gave our forests and wildlands a chance to heal, creating a false sense of security. However, after many years of suppressing fires, thus disrupting normal ecological cycles, changes in the structure and make-up of forests began to occur. Species of trees that ordinarily would have been eliminated from forests by periodic, low-intensity fires began to become a dominant part of the forest canopy. Over time, these trees became susceptible to insects and disease. Standing dead and dying trees in conjunction with other brush and downed material began to fill the forest floor. The resulting accumulation of these materials, when dried by extended periods of drought, created the fuels that promote the type of wildfires that we have seen this year.

The problems of unnaturally heavy undergrowth have been exacerbated by the introduction in the 1800s of non-native invasive weeds and grasses. These plants corrupt a region's ecological processes, robbing the soil and native plants of vital nutrients and water. Invasive species such as cheatgrass, which is pervasive on today's Western landscape, is one of the first plants to establish after a fire. It grows earlier, quicker, and higher than native grasses. Then it dies, dries, and becomes fuel. [4]

---

3 Stephen J. Pyne, *Fire in America: Cultural History of Wildland and Rural Fire*, Princeton University Press, 1982.
4 David A. Pyke, *Invasive Exotic Plants In Sagebrush Ecosystems of The Intermountain West*. Proceedings:

In short, decades of aggressive fire suppression have drastically changed the look and fire behavior of Western forests and rangelands. Forests a century ago were less dense and had larger, more fire-resistant trees. For example, in northern Arizona, some lower elevation stands of ponderosa pine that once held 50 trees per acre, now contain 200 or more trees per acre. In addition, the composition of our forests have changed from more fire-resistant tree species to non-fire resistant species such as grand fir, Douglas-fir, and subalpine fir. As a result, studies show that today's wildfires typically burn hotter, faster, and higher than those of the past.[5]

The Changing West

In addition to the unnatural fuel buildup developing in our forests and rangelands, wildland firefighting has become more complex in the last two decades due to dramatic increases in the West's population.

Of the 10 fastest-growing states in the U.S., eight are in the interior West. While the national average annual population growth is about one percent, the West has growth rates ranging from 2.5 to 13 percent.[6]

As a result, new development is occurring in fire-prone areas, often adjacent to Federal land, creating a "wildland-urban interface" -- an area where structures and other human development meet or intermingle with undeveloped wildland. This relatively new phenomenon means that more communities and structures are threatened by fire. Wildland firefighters today often spend a great deal more time and effort protecting structures than in earlier years. Consequently, firefighting has become more complicated, expensive, and dangerous.

Current Fire Management Policy

This Administration has sought to increase efforts to reduce risks associated with the buildup of fuels in forests and rangelands through a variety of approaches, including controlled burns, the physical removal of undergrowth and other unnatural concentrations of fuel, and the prevention and eradication of invasive plants. Implicit in the Administration's policy is the understanding that reversing the effects of a century of aggressive fire suppression will be an evolutionary

---

Sagebrush Steppe Ecosystems. Boise State University, Boise, Idaho.
5 J.P. Sloan 1998. *Interruption of the Natural Fire Cycle in a Grand Fir Forest of Central Idaho: Changes in Stand Structure and Composition*. Tall Timbers Fire Ecology Proceedings, No. 20. Tall Timbers Research Station, Tallahassee, Fl.
6 William E. Riebsame, Ed. *Atlas of the New West*, p. 96, W.W. Norton & Co., 1997.

process, and not one that can be completed in a few short years.

As the composition and structure of our Nation's forests have changed over time, conditions that increase the likelihood of catastrophic fire have grown. Periodic, severe wildfires have occurred when weather conditions have produced drought, dry lightning, and high winds. This was illustrated in 1988, the year of the Yellowstone fires, and in 1994, when fires claimed the lives of 34 firefighters, including 14 of our country's most elite firefighters in one inferno on Storm King Mountain in Colorado. This pattern has repeated itself in the year 2000.

After evaluating the 1988 and 1994 fires, foresters, fire ecologists, biologists, and others cautioned that the century-old policy of excluding all fires from the forests rangelands had brought about ecological changes that were increasing the likelihood of catastrophic wildfire. This was confirmed by the 1999 General Accounting Office Report, *Federal Wildfire Activities*, which noted "[F]ederal acreage is susceptible to catastrophic wildfires, particularly where the natural vegetation has been altered by past uses of the land and a century of fire suppression."[7]

Given the experiences of the 1988 and 1994 fire seasons and the recommendations of scientific experts, the Clinton/Gore Administration initiated the first-ever, comprehensive interagency review of wildland fire policy. Based on this review, which was summarized in the 1995 Federal Wildland Fire Policy Statement, the Departments of Agriculture and the Interior predicted serious and potentially permanent environmental destruction and loss of private and public resource values from large wildfires. The policy statement recognized the important function that fire plays in many ecosystems and identified the critical role fire can play in the management of forests and watersheds. The policy noted that, "[C]onditions on millions of acres of wildlands increase the probability of large, intense fires beyond any scale yet witnessed. These severe fires will in turn increase the risk to humans, to property and to the land upon which our social and economic well-being is so intimately intertwined."[8]

As three of the country's leading wildland fire ecologists recently said, "Fires will inevitably occur when we have ignitions in hot, dry, windy conditions. . . . It is one of the great paradoxes of fire suppression that the more effective we are at fire suppression, the more fuels accumulate and the more intense the next fire will be."[9]

---

7 General Accounting Office Report, *Federal Wildfire Activities,* Aug. 1999, p. 3
8 U.S. Department of Agriculture and U.S. Department of the Interior, *Federal Wildland Fire Management Policy & Program Review,* 1995 (Wildland Fire Policy)
9 Dr. Leon Nuenschwander, et al, Testimony before the Subcommittee on Forests and Forest Health, August 2000.

After the policy was put in place, the Departments dramatically increased the number of acres treated to reduce fire risks. In 1995, Federal agencies treated fewer than 500,000 acres. This year, the Departments will remove brush, small trees, and downed material from more than 2.4 million acres using small, intentionally set, "prescribed" fires and mechanical thinning techniques.

Across the country, the Departments have been working to assess the important roles that fire plays in different ecosystems and to integrate this knowledge into management practices. They also began the Joint Fire Science Project to provide a scientific basis for helping the Departments prioritize their fire prevention activities on the ground. In 1999, this project developed maps, with state-level resolution, that identify forests most at risk from large, catastrophic fires. Work continues to improve the resolution of the maps so that they can be used to help assist with strategic planning, prioritizing resources and identifying specific projects on the ground.

The Departments have been moving quickly to incorporate this new information in their budget requests and other policy documents, but the severity of this year's fire season has added extra impetus to move these recommendations forward.

III. Key Elements Of The Administration's Wildland Fire Management Policy

The new wildland fire policy that the Administration has developed in recent years acknowledges the dangers posed by the long-term building of excessive fuel levels in our forests and rangelands. It seeks to reduce those risks through a variety of approaches, including controlled burns, the physical removal of undergrowth and other unnatural concentration of fuel, and attacks on invasive plants. Implicit in the Administration's policy is the understanding that reversing the effects a century of aggressive fire suppression has had on our nation's public lands will be an evolutionary process, not one that can be completed in a few short years.

The key elements of the Administration's wildland fire management policy are set forth below. They include: (1) integrated firefighting management and preparedness; (2) reducing hazardous fuel accumulations; and (3) local community coordination and outreach.

Notably, the Administration's wildland fire policy does not rely on commercial logging or new road building to reduce fire risks and can be implemented under its current forest and land management polices. The removal of large, merchantable trees from forests does not reduce fire risk and may, in fact, increase such risk. Fire ecologists note that large trees are "insurance for the future – they are critical to ecosystem resilience."[10] Targeting smaller trees and leaving both large trees and snags standing addresses the core of the fuels problem.[11]

The Congressional Research Service (CRS) recently addressed the effect of logging on wildfires in an August 2000 report and found that the current wave of forest fires is not related to a decline in timber harvest on Federal lands. From a quantitative perspective, the CRS study indicates a very weak relationship between acres logged and the extent and severity of forest fires. To the contrary, in the most recent period (1980 through 1999) the data indicate that fewer acres burned in areas where logging activity was limited.

Since 1945, the fluctuation pattern of acres burned in the 11 Western States has shown a steady rise with some of the worst fire seasons in the late 1980's, when timber harvest peaked at 12 billion board feet. In fact, the 10-year average annual number of acres burned nationwide in the 1980's when logging activity was heaviest was higher (4.2 million acres) than in both the

---

10 Ibid.
11 Ibid.

1970's (3.2 million acres) and the 1990's (3.6 million acres).

Qualitative analysis by CRS supports the same conclusion. The CRS stated: "[T]imber harvesting removes the relatively large diameter wood that can be converted into wood products, but leaves behind the small material, especially twigs and needles. The concentration of these fine fuels on the forest floor increases the rate of spread of wildfires."[12]

Similarly, the National Research Council found that logging and clearcutting can cause rapid regeneration of shrubs and trees that can create highly flammable fuel conditions within a few years of cutting. Without adequate treatment of small woody material, logging may exacerbate fire risk rather than lower it.[13]

The President has proposed to protect more than 43 million acres of remaining National Forest roadless areas. These areas have tremendous ecological value and serve as important watersheds, areas for recreation, and important habitat for fish and wildlife.

Some critics have expressed concern that the Administration's proposed roadless area policy could increase wildfire risks. The facts do not support this conclusion. To the contrary, all available evidence suggests that fire starts may be fewer in unroaded than in previously roaded forests. Fires are almost twice as likely to occur in roaded areas as they are in roadless areas.

The proposed roadless area protection policy would not affect the Federal agencies' ability to control wildland fires. The agencies' success rate in extinguishing wildfires on initial attack is the same in roadless, wilderness, and roaded areas. Approximately 98 per cent of all fires are extinguished before the grow large and out of control. In addition, the proposed roadless policy would allow road construction if a wildland fire threatened public health and safety.

The Forest Service has identified 89 million acres of National Forest System land that have a moderate to high risk of catastrophic fire. Of these acres, less than 16 per cent are in inventoried roadless areas. Moreover, the Forest Service would prioritize efforts to reduce fuels in areas that have already been roaded because these areas tend to be much closer to communities and have higher fire risks. Indeed, given current funding levels and the scope of the fuels issue, the Forest Service would do fuels reduction work for 15 years in roaded areas.

A. Firefighting Management and Preparedness

---

12 Congressional Research Service, Memorandum to Senator Ron Wyden, "Timber Harvesting and Forest Fires," August 22, 2000.
13 Ibid.

The Administration's review of wildland fire policy validated the importance of maintaining an integrated firefighting management structure that can deliver first-class firefighting resources to the front lines of wildfires.

The Departments operate under a model interagency framework that has been developed over two decades. Program management and coordination takes place through a national-level group, the National Wildfire Coordination Group, which includes representatives from the States. It determines training, equipment, and other standards to ensure that all Federal, State, and local agencies can easily operate together.

The fire program operates under a command structure called Incident Command System to respond to and manage wildfires on an intergovernmental basis. The system includes local fire operations that are supported by a national network of coordination centers and supply bases. The National Interagency Fire Center in Boise, Idaho, oversees national wildfire operations.

The Administration has provided full support to the interagency firefighting effort (see attachment A) and has implemented a series of budget and management improvements.

Based on lessons of recent fire seasons, especially 1999 and 2000, the Departments have reassessed the assumptions and variables used in planning models to determine the resources needed to fight fires. They recommend funding 100 percent of this revised estimate of full preparedness.

In addition, the Departments have devoted special attention to firefighting training and coordination. As part of this emphasis, the Departments have added training courses, modified current classes, and, in some cases, raised the qualifications for certain positions. In 1999, the Departments issued a revised qualifications system for firefighting and prescribed fire positions in order to ensure that the U.S. continues to field the finest firefighting and prescribed fire force in the world.

B. Reducing Hazardous Fuel Accumulations

Implicit in the Administration's efforts to reduce wildfire risk through the elimination of brush, small diameter trees, and other fuels and the reintroduction of fire to forest and rangeland ecosystems is the understanding that reversing the effects a century of aggressive fire suppression will be an evolutionary process, not one that can be completed in a few short years.

The Administration's forest policies have emphasized the importance of reducing hazardous fuel accumulations in our forests and rangelands and restoring the health and natural processes of forest and rangeland ecosystems. Reduction of fuels can be achieved in a variety of ways -- by mechanical, chemical, biological and manual methods. The prudent use of fire, either alone or in combination with other means, can be one of the most effective means of reducing such hazardous fuel. In addition, early research has demonstrated that the selective removal of undergrowth and non-native plant species, can significantly reduce fire risks. The Administration is testing the effectiveness of these strategies' pilot projects.

By way of example, in a report published in *Proceedings from the Joint Fire Science Conference and Workshop, 1991*,[14] researchers studied four large wildfires in Montana, Washington, California, and Arizona to determine if previous fuel treatment and thinning activities had any impact on fire severity. The sites selected for study underwent treatment within ten years prior to being burned in wildland fires. The findings indicated that fuel treatments mitigate fire severity. "Although topography and weather may play a more important role in fuels in governing fire behavior, topography and weather cannot be realistically manipulated to reduce fire severity. Fuels are the leg of the fire environment triangle that land managers can change to achieve desired post-fire condition."

The General Accounting Office (GAO Report GAO/RCED-99-65) also has emphasized the need for fuels management, concluding that "the most extensive and serious problem related to the health of forests in the interior West is the over-accumulation of vegetation, which has caused an increasing number of large, intense, uncontrollable, and catastrophically destructive wildfires."

The Departments have moved forward with an aggressive program to thin forest stands to reduce small diameter trees, underbrush and accumulated fuels

Between 1994 and this year, the Departments increased their efforts to reduce fire risks through prescribed fire and thinning by close to 500 percent (see attachment B). In 1999, the Departments treated 2.2 million acres. At the same time, the Departments have increased the use of prescribed fires to begin steering our forests and rangelands back toward more healthy conditions.

---

14 J. Polet and P. Omi, *The Effects of Thinning and Prescribed Burning on Wildland Fire Severity in Ponderosa Pini Forests,* 1999.

Presently, both Departments are developing strategies to address aggressive fuel management. These call for a targeted approach to removing excessive fuel through mechanical treatments and prescribed fire in order to protect communities at risk, help prevent insect and disease damage, and generally improve overall ecosystem health and sustainability. Obviously, large-scale improvements will take several years to occur against the backdrop of a century-long suppression policy. Nonetheless, this year's fire season is providing some evidence that the controlled reintroduction of fire is beginning to bear fruit.

An example involves a wildfire in South Dakota's Black Hills. The Jasper fire, more than 82,000 acres, is the largest fire in the history of the Black Hills. It has displayed the most severe fire behavior in the history of the area, burning 50,000 acres in only a few hours. During the course of a fierce crown -- fire run -- where flames roar through the forest through the tops of the trees -- the fire burned into a section of the Jewel Cave National Park where a prescribed fire had been conducted near the Park's visitor center and housing area. When it hit the prescribed burn area, the fire changed from a crown-fire to a ground-based fire where it could be effectively fought. Fire crews were able to remain in the area only because of the defensible space and barriers created. As a result, none of the Park's major structures burned.

As dramatic as this example is, an equally dramatic example illustrates the risks that are inherent in prescribed fires if they are not implemented in a careful and well-managed manner.

Specifically, the Cerro Grande fire near New Mexico's Los Alamos National Laboratory, which began as a prescribed fire in Bandelier National Park in New Mexico in May, is a terrible reminder of the costs if prescribed fires are not well-planned and executed. Nearly 300 homes were damaged or destroyed, 18,000 people were evacuated, and 48,000 acres were burned. The Administration fully supported a compensation program enacted by Congress for the victims of the fire. The Administration is also fully committed to implementing changes in prescribed fire policy and procedures as a result of investigations and reviews of the Cerro Grande fire.

C. Local Community Coordination and Outreach

The Administration's wildland fire policy recognizes that effective fire management requires close coordination with local communities, particularly those communities that are in the wildland-urban interface. As the management of private lands has become a key factor in the fire-risk equation, the Departments have recognized the importance of providing outreach, education, and support for local communities who must play a primary role in reducing fire hazards in and near their communities.

As discussed above, the changing demographics are expanding the wildland-urban interface and creating new challenges for fighting wildland fires. Increasingly, many homes on private land in and around new communities are at risk. Indeed, the National Fire Protection Association (NFPA) estimates that wildfires destroyed more than 9,000 homes between 1985 and 1995. Officials further believe that the number of homes damaged by wildfires in the 1990s is six times that of the previous decade. More than 1,000 homes have been destroyed during this summer alone.

Safe and effective protection in these areas demands close coordination between local, State, Federal and Tribal firefighting resources. Typically, the primary burden for wildland-urban interface fire protection falls to property owners and State and local governments. Rural and volunteer fire departments provide the front line of defense, or initial attack, on up to 90 percent of these high-risk and costly fires. While they have a good record in rapidly suppressing traditional wildland fires, these local resources often struggle to effectively address the complex demands of fighting fire in the wildland-urban interface.

The Departments also have taken steps to assist communities in developing their own firefighting capabilities. The Forest Service's State and Volunteer Fire Assistance Programs, for example, provide technical and financial assistance to local firefighting resources to help promote effective and coordinated integrated fire management response. Through the Volunteer Fire Assistance Program, the Forest Service has been successful in providing firefighting equipment to rural fire departments and in training their firefighters to meet Federal interagency standards.

The Departments have made available the training facilities at the National Interagency Training Center in Boise, Idaho, to community-based firefighters. By way of example, the BLM Boise District in Idaho has trained more than 1,500 firefighters from 57 different fire departments from both urban (e.g. Boise) and rural areas within the last five years. Training opportunities recently have been extended to ranchers who are interested in fire proofing their properties and understanding basic fire suppression tactics. The Boise District also has formalized an agreement with Ada County, Idaho, to train and integrate county employees into certain firefighting operations and promote an effective and coordinated integrated fire management response.

The problem of fires in the wildland-urban interface is multifaceted and will not be solved overnight. Nevertheless, there are a number of short-term actions that the Federal government, in cooperation with State, tribal and local governments, can take to reduce the future risk to communities and resources.

A top priority for reducing risk is to reduce fuels in forests and rangelands adjacent to, and within communities. Particular emphasis should be placed on projects where fuel treatment can also be accomplished on adjoining State, private, or other nonfederal land so as to extend greater protection across the landscape. This provides protection from catastrophic fires that develop on public lands. This can be accomplished by making available adequate incentives and technical assistance to communities and private landowners to encourage the reduction of hazardous fuels around homeowner properties. These individual actions will not only provide greater personal protection but will also increase the safety and effectiveness of firefighting personnel. When done on a large scale, fuel reduction around individual homes can result in greater overall protection for an entire landscape or watershed.

The Departments have been implementing a number of programs to educate communities and homeowners in recently burned areas and high-risk urban-wildland interface areas about fire hazards. The Forest Service's Firewise program, for example, is a very successful program designed to educate rural homeowners about precautions they can take to make their homes more fire resistant and more easily defendable by local fire departments. Firewise specifically helps communities and homeowners recognize fire hazards, design Firewise homes and landscapes, and make wise planning, zoning, and building material choices. These efforts play an important role in reducing the loss of lives and property -- as well as tremendous government expense -- in the wildland-urban interface.

III. Consequences of the 2000 Wildfire Season

Economic Impacts

Although the data needed for a thorough assessment of economic impacts on areas affected by this year's wildfires are not yet available, preliminary reports indicate that the losses from the 2000 wildfires will be substantial and widespread. Montana Governor Racicot estimated that businesses were losing about $3 million a day because of fire. Idaho Governor Kempthorne estimated losses in Idaho at $54.1 million overall, of which $15 million comes from about 500 small businesses. He estimated another $12.5 million in agricultural losses and $12 million in watershed restoration costs.

Economic impacts arise both directly from fire damage and indirectly from changes in local economic activity, such as a drop in tourism. Both direct and indirect effects of the wildfires have exacted a heavy economic toll on many local, often rural communities.

In Hamilton, Montana, the loss of more than 300,000 acres to fire prompted officials to close much of the public land essential to Montana's tourism economy. As a result, the Chamber of Commerce reports that seven chamber members alone had reported losses totaling $500,000. A local fishing guide who relies on tourists told reporters that he had lost 76 percent of his normal business in one month alone.[15]

In Idaho, two ranchers lost more than 700 cattle during a 20,000-acre fire near Dietrich, with a value of at least half a million dollars. Insurance will cover about 25 percent for one of the ranchers. The other rancher had no insurance on his herds.[16]

President Clinton responded to requests from the Governors of Idaho and Montana and declared the two states as disaster areas, making them eligible for Federal relief. One-stop centers are being established so that citizens can obtain service and financial assistance from all relevant agencies.

Damage to Natural Resources

---

15 CNN News, September 3, 2000
16 *Idaho Statesman*, August 24, 2000

In addition to these types of direct, out-of-pocket impacts on citizens, it is likely that losses in resource values will total billions of dollars.

The consequences of this year's wildfires on our country's natural resources are as vast as they are varied. The wildland fires of 2000 fires have burned both public and private lands over a broad spectrum of semi-arid rangeland and forested ecosystems, often encompassing entire watersheds critical to community water supplies. Compared to historic fire events, recent fires have burned with such intensity that the ecosystems of many of these extensively burned areas have been drastically changed. Without intervention, these burned lands will recover slowly and be susceptible to undesirable changes in vegetation composition. For example, plant species such as cheatgrass often become established in burned areas, creating additional fire risks and disrupting natural systems.

The immediate problems associated with the severity of fire will extend well into winter. With a lack of vegetation on hillsides, for example, the likelihood that rain and snowfall will create flooding and mudslides increases. In turn, the water quality of streams and rivers are damaged, which can kill native fish. Many wildlife populations also have been killed or disrupted.

Non-native invasive plant species -- weeds -- thrive on both public and private lands in the wake of wildland fires, presenting several problems. These opportunistic plants compete with and can overtake native plant communities. In addition, their proliferation provides powerful fuel for wildfires, increasing the likelihood of and severity of future wildfires. Cheatgrass, in particular, has spread throughout the West on degraded rangelands, increasing in density on burned areas. In the Great Basin ecosystem alone, one out of every three acres is either dominated or threatened by cheatgrass.

Harvesting Burned Trees

The appropriate harvest of fire-damaged timber can provide a means of recovering some of the economic value of forest stands and improving landscape health, but it is not a panacea for reducing wildfire risk. Removal activities that do not comply with environmental requirements can add to the damage associated with fire-impacted landscapes.

The Departments will continue to consider the option of harvesting fire-damaged trees when appropriate, with priority placed on those areas where roads already exist and where risks to communities from future wildfire are greatest. However, as has been the Departments' practice, such timber sales should proceed only after all environmental laws and procedures are followed and the affected communities are afforded the opportunity to participate in the process.

In the past, some Congressionally mandated salvage logging resulted in the harvest of green, healthy trees in addition to dead and dying timber. Congressional direction contained in the 1995 Rescissions Act -- known as the "Salvage Rider" -- placed priority on salvage logging over environmental protection. This is not an acceptable approach to harvesting fire-damaged trees.

IV. Key Points and Recommendations

1. Continue to Make All Necessary Firefighting Resources Available.

As a first priority, the Departments will continue to provide all necessary resources to ensure that fire suppression efforts are at maximum efficiency in order to protect life and property. The United States' wildland firefighting organization is the finest in the world and deserves our strong support. To ensure continued readiness of the firefighting force, the Departments recommend providing additional resources for firefighting activities.

Wildland firefighting is a difficult and dangerous job, and it is essential that our firefighters continue to be well trained, with the appropriate equipment and resources they need to do their job. Safety of our firefighters and members of the public is, and always will be, the Administration's number one priority. We will continue to provide all necessary resources that our firefighting force need to continue the battle against this year's fires in as safe a manner as possible.

To fully fund the fire management preparedness programs, the Departments recommend additional resources in FY 2001 of about $337 million, including $204 million for the Forest Service and $133 million for the Department of the Interior over the President's request. This continuing funding would provide the Departments' fire management organizations with the capability to prevent, detect, and take prompt, effective action to control wildfires. These funds also would support the personnel, equipment, and technology necessary to conduct proper planning, prevention, detection, information, education, and training.

2. Restore Damaged Landscapes and Rebuild Communities.

After ensuring that suppression resources are sufficient, invest in the restoration of communities and landscapes impacted by the year 2000 fires. The Departments also recommend that investments in the treatment of landscapes through thinning and the restoration of fire be continued and expanded to help reduce the risk of catastrophic fires.

Providing Economic Assistance to Hard-Hit Communities

As discussed above, the year 2000 fires have hit many communities hard. Both the Federal Emergency Management Agency (FEMA) and the Small Business Administration (SBA) are responding to the immediate need for assistance. FEMA anticipates that more than 10,000 citizens from Idaho and Montana may qualify for disaster unemployment assistance, and it is anticipated that the SBA may offer more than $50 million in small business loans to assist affected businessmen. The USDA's Forest Service and rural development program also are preparing to provide immediate economic assistance, using existing resources. In receiving grant or loan applications under these programs, the Department of Agriculture will fully consider the impact of the season's wildfires on communities seeking assistance, giving such communities a competitive advantage in the USDA grant-making and loan-making.

In addition to these short-term actions, the Departments recommend that stabilization and restoration investments be made in areas that have been damaged by fire and which are at risk of erosion, invasive species germination or water supply contamination. These investments should be made in a manner that provides maximum benefit to hard-hit communities with local contractors and the local workforce being utilized to maximum extent possible.

In a similar vein, the Departments also are recommending below that forest treatment activities be stepped up in intensity. These activities can be labor intensive and, once again, the Departments intend to involve local communities and the local workforce in implementing these activities.

Key aspects of these programs are set forth below.

Burned Area Stabilization and Restoration

Stabilization

Stabilization activities include short-term actions to remove hazards and stabilize soils and slopes. Examples of specific actions or "treatments" might include the removal of hazards; seeding by helicopter, plane, or by hand; constructing dams or other structures to hold soil on the slope; placing bundles of straw on the ground, parallel to the slope to slow the movement of soil down hill; contour furrowing or trenching (ditches cut into the mountain or hillsides to catch soil moving down hill); correcting road drainage by realigning poorly designed roads and culvert replacement to manage water and soil movement after the fire; and temporarily fencing cattle and people out of burned areas.

Priorities for stabilization activities include protecting human life and property; protecting public health and safety; stabilizing municipal watersheds; stabilizing steep slopes and unstable terrain; protecting archeological resources; and replacing culverts.

Restoration

Restoration activities include longer-term actions to repair or improve lands that are unlikely to recover naturally from severe fire damage. Examples of specific actions or "treatments" might include planting or seeding native species; reforesting desired tree species; chemical or mechanical treatment to reduce competition; and other efforts to limit the spread of invasive species.

Priorities for restoration activities include preventing introduction of non-native invasive species; promoting restoration of ecosystem structure and composition; rehabilitating threatened and endangered species habitat; and improving water quality.

> Because of the large amount of acreage affected by this year's fires, the Departments propose to develop a stabilization and restoration plan that is coordinated with all affected agencies, including appropriate state and local agencies.

> Responsibility for implementation of individual projects lies at the field-level. Projects covering multiple jurisdictions will be planned and implemented on an interagency basis.

The Departments recognize that the scope of this effort will require additional resources. Three specific aspects of the program may require special support:

(1)   *Native plant/seed sources:* Availability of native seeds and plant materials is limited. Significant effort will be needed to encourage the production of seeds and plant materials by the private sector and develop agency seed storage capabilities to support restoration activities.

(2)   *Science and research:* Significant information collection, research, and data analysis is required to assess the effectiveness of restoration techniques and develop improved techniques. Current technologies and techniques are largely based on experiences from agricultural practices in the early part of the 20th Century. Special attention will be focused on techniques applicable to non-agricultural lands and to treatments using native seeds and plants.

(3)   *Capital equipment:* The current post-fire program relies on a limited amount of capital equipment (e.g., drill-seeders), much of which is not dedicated to this program. Additional equipment will be needed to support the expanded requirements, especially in the application of native seeds.

3. Investments in Projects to Reduce Fire Risk

As discussed above, the Departments have been implementing new approaches to address the long-term buildup of hazardous fuels in our forests and rangelands. The fires of 2000 have underscored the importance of pursuing an aggressive program to address the fuels problem with the help of local communities, particularly those in wildland-urban interface areas, where threats to lives and property are greater and the complexity and costs of treatments higher.

The Departments recommend continuing current fuel reduction strategies and seeking additional budgetary resources to treat additional acreage. The Departments are requesting $257 million for fuels reduction activities in FY 2001, over the President's request including $115 million for the Forest Service and $142 million for the Department of the Interior. These funds will cover accelerated treatments, especially in the wildland-urban interface area and will work to support additional research and eradication of invasive species. Funding will be available to support Endangered Species Act consultation work by the U.S. Fish and Wildlife Service and the National Marine Fisheries Service.

Implementation of Fuels Reduction Program

The most significant implementation challenge for the Departments is to substantially increase the number of acres of forestlands that receive fuels treatment. Both Departments are utilizing one aspect of fuels treatments, prescribed fires, increasingly. That program will continue to play a key role, although the lessons from the Cerro Grande fire demand that this strategy be implemented with great care. In that regard, the Departments will implement recommendations from the independent review of the Cerro Grande fire.

In addition to prescribed burns, the physical removal of undergrowth and other fuels needs to be stepped up in intensity in order to have a more significant impact on dangerous fuels buildup. Because of the importance of this activity, the Departments recommend that experienced personnel be dedicated full time to this activity, with direct chains of command to the Secretaries of Agriculture and the Interior. The Secretaries, in turn, should meet periodically to assess the progress of these efforts.

Markets for Removed Materials

Because much of the hazardous fuels in forests are excessive levels of forest-based biomass -- dead, diseased and down trees -- and small diameter trees, there are several benefits of finding economical uses for this material, including helping offset forest restoration cost; providing economic opportunities for rural, forest-dependent communities; reducing the risks from catastrophic wildfires; protecting watersheds; helping restore forest resiliency, and protecting the environment.

USDA Forest Service research teams are working to develop new uses for small tress and new ways to process them. A need exists to transfer and commercialize new technology as it comes on line and to develop and expand local markets for these products. Both Departments propose to partner with communities, universities, and businesses to conduct additional research on the stimulation of small diameter and other vegetative products industries.

Small diameter logs, for example, can be used for housing material such as trim, siding, and sub-flooring. Recent technology now makes it possible for wood composites - fibers, flakes and strands - from lower quality species of trees such as juniper, pinyon pine, and insect-killed white fir to be used successfully for particleboard and replacement filler for thermoplastic composites that make up a wide range of consumer products such as highway signs. Similar uses are being expanded for pulp chips. The woody residues that make up a forest's undergrowth has historically been burned or allowed to accumulate in huge piles on the forest floor. This material could potentially be economically used as compost and mulch material.

Research Needs

Given the severity of this year's fires and the additional fuels management and restoration activities recommended by this report, the Departments have a number of additional research needs. They recommend research on the relationship between invasive species and fires and the effectiveness of various treatment efforts. They also recommend research based on recent fire seasons regarding relationships between land management practices and the occurrence and intensity of fires.

Budget

The two Departments request additional resources of $130 million in FY 2001 over the President's request to fully fund a burned area restoration program as described above, including $45 million for the Forest Service and $85 million for the Department of the Interior.

4. Work Directly with Local Communities.

Working with local communities is a critical element in restoring damaged landscapes and reducing fire hazards proximate to homes and communities. To accomplish this, the Departments recommend:

a. **Expanding the participation of local communities in efforts to reduce fire hazards and the use of local labor for fuels treatment and restoration work.**

b. **Improving local fire protection capabilities through financial and technical assistance to state, local, and volunteer firefighting efforts.**

c. **Assisting in the development of markets for traditionally underutilized small diameter wood as a value added outlet for removed fuels.**

d. **Encouraging a dialogue within and among communities regarding opportunities for reducing wildfire risk and expanding outreach and education to homeowners and communities about fire prevention through use of programs such as Firewise.**

As discussed above, the Departments have been working with communities on fire-related activities through a variety of programs. On the operational side, the National Interagency Fire Center provides training opportunities for local firefighters, and the Fire Center has developed cooperative arrangements with many local and state entities to facilitate coordinated firefighting efforts. The Departments also work with local communities to assist in fire protection activities through the Firewise program and other outreach efforts. In addition, the Departments currently work with local communities on fuels treatment and post-fire restoration projects.

Although Federal agencies are engaged in these activities on an on-going basis, the Departments recommend that a significant new initiative be undertaken to coordinate appropriate investments and outreach activities with affected communities. The proposed initiative would focus on three major arenas: (1) improving community-based firefighting capabilities and coordination with state and Federal firefighting efforts; (2) working closely with communities-at-risk in implementing post-fire restoration activities and fuels reduction activities; and (3) expanding joint education and outreach efforts regarding fire prevention and mitigation in the wildlife-urban interface.

Rural and volunteer fire departments provide the front line of defense, or initial attack, on up to 90 percent of the communities. Volunteer fire departments are the backbone of fire protection in America. County, State, and Federal agencies provide immediate backup to local fire departments when a wildland-urban interface fire gets out of control. Strong readiness capability at the state and local levels go hand-in-hand with optimal efficiency at the Federal level. The level of funding being proposed will provide a more optimum efficiency level for the states and local fire departments in the impacted areas.

Budget

To support this initiative for community involvement and participation, additional funding of $88 million in FY 2001 is required. The USDA Forest Service proposes increases of $53.8 million for state and volunteer fire assistance, as well as an additional $12.5 million for economic action programs and $12 million for forest health activity. The Department of the Interior proposes a new program to support rural fire districts, particularly those intermingled with Bureau of Land Management lands. Funding of $10 million is proposed for FY 2001.

5. Be Accountable

A Cabinet-level management structure should be established to ensure that the actions recommended by the Departments receive the highest priority. The Secretaries of Agriculture and the Interior should co-chair this effort. Regional integrated management teams should be accountable for fuels treatment, restoration, and fire preparedness. Local teams, working closely with communities and other agency partners, would manage projects on the ground.

Wildland fires know no jurisdictional boundaries. It is for that reason that the five primary Federal agencies that have operational responsibility for preparing for, and responding to, wildfires, formed the National Interagency Fire Center. The Fire Center is a model of cross-agency cooperation and accountability, and it provides a key focal point for coordination with state and local firefighting efforts.

As with fighting fires, Federal, State and local governments will have to cooperate to restore damaged lands, invest in protecting affected communities, and reduce hazardous fuel loads.

A number of existing, regional integrated management teams are in place to assist in the setting of regional priorities for land restoration, fuels treatment, and community cooperation and outreach. The Departments recommend that these regional structures be utilized and/or retooled, as appropriate, to provide a focal point for these initiatives.

The Departments would also establish locally led teams with the Department of Commerce and other appropriate agencies. These integrated teams would identify specific land restoration, fuels treatment, and preparedness projects; coordinate environmental reviews and consultations; facilitate and encourage public participation; and monitor and evaluate project implementation.

Because of the critical importance of these matters, the Departments recommend Cabinet-level oversight of the implementation of these initiatives, co-chaired by the Secretaries of Agriculture and the Interior. Among other things, the new management team would be responsible for ensuring that appropriate performance objectives are established and met, ensuring that adequate financial and other resources are made available, establishing a system for identifying and addressing implementation issues promptly, and ensuring that the environmental reviews required by the National Environmental Policy Act, and all other environmental requirements, are undertaken and completed on a timely basis.

The Departments recommend that the Cabinet-level group assess the progress towards implementing these tasks, and provide periodic reports to the President.

Appendix: Funding Summary

Nearly $1.6 billion in additional resources over the President's FY2001 Budget requests for the USDA Forest Service and the US Department of the Interior will be required in FY 2001 to meet the objectives of this report. This includes $897 million more for the USDA Forest Service, and $682 million more for the US Department of the Interior.

To continue the momentum gained by the additional FY 2001 resources, future funding for fiscal year 2002 and the out years will need to be maintained for these same program components. Tables 1 through 3 summarize these needs for FY2001, by totals and by each Department.

Table 1
FY 2001 Funding Summary, USDA Forest Service and the US Department of the Interior

USDA Forest Service and the US DOI	FY 2000 Final	FY 2001 President's Budget	FY 2001 Additional Needs	FY 2001 Total Needs	FY 2001 House Action	FY 2001 Senate Action
			...Dollars in thousands...			
Fire Preparedness	$584,618	$586,433	$336,381	$922,814	$586,433	$586,683
Fire Operations	323,995	331,136	677,711	1,008,847	320,107	579,394
Emergency Fire Contingency	290,000	150,000	476,000	626,000	200,000	150,000
State Fire Assistance	23,929	30,006	42,994	73,000	25,000	28,042
Volunteer Fire Assistance	3,240	2,510	10,790	13,300	5,000	5,000
Rural Fire Assistance	0	0	10,000	10,000	0	0
Forest Health Management	62,075	62,842	12,000	74,842	63,794	63,383
Economic Action Programs	20,198	17,267	12,500	29,767	14,246	23,486
TOTAL	$1,308,055	$1,180,194	$1,578,376	$2,758,570	$1,214,580	$1,435,988

Table 2.
FY 2001 Funding Summary, USDA Forest Service

USDA Forest Service	FY 2000 Final	FY 2001 President's Budget	FY 2001 Additional Needs	FY 2001 Total Needs	FY 2001 House Action	FY 2001 Senate Action
			...Dollars in thousands...			
Fire Preparedness	$408,768	$404,343	$203,547	$607,890	$404,343	$404,593
Fire Operations	208,888	216,029	338, 971	555,000	210,000	333,300
Emergency Fire Contingency	90,000	150,000	276,000	426,000	0	150,000
State Fire Assistance	23,929	30,006	42,994	73,000	25,000	28,042
Volunteer Fire Assistance	3,240	2,510	10,790	13,300	5,000	5,000
Rural Fire Assistance	0	0	0	0	0	0
Forest Health Management	62,075	62,842	12,000	74,842	63,794	63,383
Economic Action Programs	20,198	17,267	12,500	29,767	14,246	23,486
TOTAL	**$817,098**	**$882,997**	**$896,802**	**$1,779,799**	**$722,383**	**$1,007,804**

Table 3
FY 2001 Funding Summary, US Department of the Interior

US Department of the Interior	FY 2000 Final	FY 2001 President's Budget	FY 2001 Additional Needs	FY 2001 Total Needs	FY 2001 House Action	FY 2001 Senate Action
			...Dollars in thousands...			
Fire Preparedness	$175,850	$182,090	$132,834	$314,924	$182,090	$182,090
Fire Operations	115,107	115,107	338,740	453,847	110,107	246,094
Emergency Fire Contingency	200,000	0	200,000	200,000	200,000	0
State Fire Assistance**	0	0	0	0	0	0
Volunteer Fire Assistance**	0	0	0	0	0	0
Rural Fire Assistance*	0	0	10,000	10,000	0	0
Forest Health Management**	0	0	0	0	0	0
Economic Action Programs**	0	0	0	0	0	0
TOTAL	**$490,957**	**$297,197**	**$681,574**	**$978,771**	**$492,197**	**$428,184**

*New program proposed in the Report to the President
** No DOI equivalent to these USDA Forest Service programs

The following briefly describes each program component, including total funding requirements for FY 2001 (President's request plus additional resources now being requested):

Fire Preparedness
Provides the fire management organization with the capability to prevent, detect, or take prompt, effective initial attack suppression action on wildfires. Preparedness activities include planning, prevention, detection, information and education, pre-incident training, equipment and supply purchase and replacement, and other preparedness activities. Funding estimates are

based on prediction models that determine a cost-effective level of preparedness for initial and extended attack.

- For the USDA Forest Service $608 million for recurring readiness and program management costs, including fire science and research.
- For the US Department of the Interior $315 million for recurring readiness and program management costs; one-time readiness and program management costs; fire science and research; and fire management facilities repair.

Fire Operations - Suppression

Provides costs directly associated with fire suppression activities (personnel costs, contracts, aviation, supplies, and so on)

- For the USDA Forest Service $320 million.
- For US Department of the Interior $153 million.

Fire Operations – Fuels Management

Use of prescribed fire, mechanical removal, and other techniques to remove/reduce hazardous levels of fuels in order to reduce risks to communities and to restore natural fire regimes to wildlands. Includes funding to support non-fire disciplines (biology, wildlife, hydrologists, etc.) necessary to conduct planning and assessment activities.

- For the USDA Forest Service $190 million including $20 million for research and $11.5 million to support environmental clearances.
- For US Department of the Interior $195 million, including at least $20 million to support environmental clearances.

Fire Operations – Burned Area Rehabilitation

Provides for post-fire stabilization and restoration of burned lands. Short-term stabilization efforts remove hazards and address erosion, flooding, and mudslide problems. Longer-term rehabilitation are targeted on those portions of fires that burned severely, thus less likely to revegetate naturally. Special attention focused on lands subject to non-native, invasive species.

- For the USDA Forest Service $45 million.
- For US Department of the Interior $105 million.
- Both Departments will have flexibility to increase these levels if estimated needs in other fire-related activities are less than currently projected.

Emergency Fire Contingency

Provides additional emergency funds for Fire Suppression activities that are only released to the agency upon Presidential declaration that regular suppression funds are insufficient. These funds ensure that funding is always available to fight wildfires.

- For the USDA Forest Service $426 million, of which $276 is to repay the Knutsen-Vandenberg (K-V) Fund.
- For US Department of the Interior $200 million, including estimated $75 million to repay a September 2000 Section 102 transfer.

State and Volunteer Fire Assistance

State fire assistance in the USDA Forest Service provides technical training, financial assistance, and equipment to States to ensure that Federal, State, and local agencies can deliver a uniform and coordinated suppression response to wildfire. Special emphasis will be placed on a Wildland-Urban Interface component.

- For the USDA Forest Service $86 million including $20 million for incentives for high priority forest management practices on their lands to reduce fire risk and fuel loads and $4 million for high priority fire education and prevention programs in the wildland-urban interface.
- US Department of the Interior has no equivalent program; see Rural Fire Assistance program below.

Rural Fire Assistance

Rural fire district assistance in the Department of the Interior is a new program to provide technical and financial support to volunteer fire departments that protect communities with populations of less than 10,000. Emphasis is on areas intermingled with lands managed by the Interior Department (especially the Bureau of Land Management).

- USDA Forest Service has no equivalent program; see State and Volunteer Fire Assistance above.
- For US Department of the Interior $10 million.

Forest Health Management

Provides forest health technical and financial assistance to all Federal agencies, Tribal governments, and States in carrying out a coordinated nationwide program of detecting, monitoring, evaluating, preventing and suppressing invasive forest insects and diseases.

- For the USDA Forest Service $75 million, including funding for the management and control of invasive species as a result of the fires and are based on estimates of detection, evaluation, and high priority management and control treatments.
- US Department of the Interior has no equivalent program.

Economic Action Program

Provides technical and financial assistance to address the long-term health of rural areas, by helping communities develop opportunities and enterprises through diversified uses of forest resources.

- For the USDA Forest Service $30 million, including funding for rural community assistance, forest products conservation and recycling, and market development and expansion.
- US Department of the Interior has no equivalent program.

Attachment A

Wildland Preparedness Funding History

Department of the Interior and USDA Forest Service

(BA in millions)

	FY 1999 Enacted	FY 2000 Enacted	FY 2001 Request
Department of the Interior	$157	$176	$182
USDA Forest Service	325	360	404 *
Total	**$482**	**$536**	**$586**

* BA reflects the revised USDA Forest Service budget structure in FY 2001

Attachment B

Acres Treated

Year	USDA Forest Service	Department of the Interior
	Acres in Thousands	
1993	385	368
1994	384	334
1995	570	348
1996	617	298
1997	1,097	503
1998	1,489	620
1999	1,412	765